HOW TO
AND DO IT WELL

A Guide For Catching More Fish For All Ages

CONTENTS

Pictures in this book come "ALIVE"
with the AUGMENTED REALITY APP

Download the
FREE IOS APP
HOW TO FISH AR

BY FINLEY W. KETCHUM
ILLUSTRATED BY JOHN R. SPEETER

12 WAYS TO CATCH MORE FISH

MATCH YOUR FISHING REEL TO THE PROPER FISHING ROD

 A spinning or underspin reel sits below on a spinning rod. A push button spin cast or a bait casting reel sits above on a bait casting rod. Choose a rod with a sensitive flexible light action for panfish. Use a stiffer heavier action rod for gamefish. The action of the rod and suggested line weights are written on each rod above the grip. Match your rod action to the species of fish you plan to catch.

Bait Casting Reel

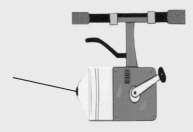

Underspin Reel

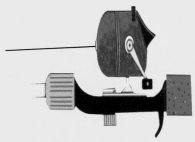

Push Button Reel

Spinning Reel

#2

USE A QUALITY CLEAR LINE THAT HAS RESISTANCE TO COILING AND TWISTING

A limp twist free line will cast further and have better knot strength. Change your line often. Always use the smallest diameter, lowest pound test line possible. Use 2 to 4 pound test line to catch panfish. Tie your fishing line directly to your hook or lure. Do not use swivels, snaps, or large sinkers.

#3

PRESENT YOUR BAIT IN A NATURAL LIFELIKE MANNER

Fish can see better than you think. Cover the whole hook with bait.

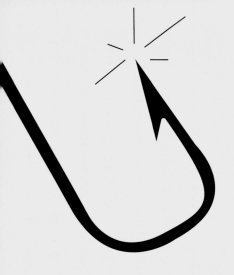

#4

KEEP HOOKS SHARP

Sharpen all your hooks to catch more fish. When a fish is biting the bait and tugging your line, quickly snap your wrist up to set the hook. Then start reeling in your fish.

#5

LEARN TO TIE A FISHING KNOT THAT DOES NOT SLIP AND HAS GOOD STRENGTH

The uni knot is the most common knot used by successful fisher people.

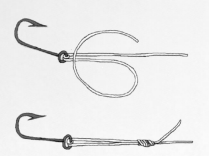

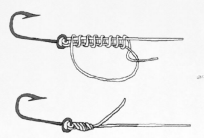

IT'S EASY TO GET HOOKED ON FISHIN'....

#6

FRESH LIVE BAIT WILL INCREASE YOUR FISHING SUCCESS

Wax worms, leaf worms, crickets, wigglers (mayfly larvae), or small minnows are great baits for all species of panfish. Night crawlers and 4 to 5 inch shiner minnows are used for catching larger fish, such as bass, walleye, and pike.

#7

FINDING FISH

Fish are cold-blooded. Water temperature affects their activity level and feeding habits. Cold water holds more dissolved oxygen than warm water. Fish will be found in cool shallow water during the winter, spring, and fall. During the warm summer, fish will move deeper to find cooler water. Fish will often suspend at different depths in deeper water.

#8

ALWAYS WEAR A QUALITY PAIR OF POLARIZED SUNGLASSES AND WIDE BRIM/LONG BILL HAT WHEN OUT FISHING

Polarized sunglasses reduce glare and eye strain. They help you see fish and bottom structures under the water.

#9

KEEP YOUR HANDS CLEAN

Fish can smell. Keep your hands free of gasoline, suntan oils, and insect repellents when handling bait or lures. Clean hands catch more fish!

#10

ANCHOR YOUR BOAT

Bring an anchor that has at least 50 feet of rope length and is heavy enough to hold your boat. Keep your boat from drifting away from the fish.

#11

WHEN TO FISH

Fish movement, location, and feeding times are based on the amount of sunlight in a 24 hour period. Fish tend to feed most often during the low light conditions of early morning or evening. During peak sunlight, try fishing near shaded areas or weed beds that provide fish with shadows and cover.

#12

FISHING WITH JIGS

Up your catch by using flashy, glittery jigs. A jig is a hook with a molded weight of lead, tungsten, or ceramic. Jigs are made to imitate the natural foods fish feed upon, such as minnows and aquatic insect larvae. Start by jiggling or hopping the jig off the lake or stream bottom. Then twitch the jig up the water column to where fish may be suspended. Cover the jig's hook with live bait to get more bites.

KNOW YOUR FISH

A simple way to classify fish is to call them panfish or gamefish. The term panfish is used for smaller fish less than 10 inches in length. Gamefish are larger fish, usually caught for sport and then released.

PANFISH

What is a panfish? A panfish is a general term used for small edible fish including bluegill, sunfish, perch, crappie, trout, and rock bass. These fish are incredibly delicious when caught from cold, clean, deep waters.

BLUEGILL

Bluegills have a distinct, solid, black spot on the back edge of their gill covers. These fish are most often found near edges of weed beds 10 to 15 feet deep. In the spring they move to more shallow water to lay their eggs. To catch Bluegills and other panfish, use a 5'6" to 6' light action rod with an underspin reel filled with 3 pound test clear line. The best baits are leaf worms, wax worms, leeches, and crickets. They are great tasting fish.

YELLOW PERCH

Yellow Perch have long greenish gold bodies with dark vertical bands. Their bellies are pearl white and sometimes marked with bright orange. Use care when handling these fish. They have very sharp spines on their backs and one or more spines on their gill covers. Perch travel in schools and are aggressive nibblers and biters. They are usually found in waters less than 20 feet deep near natural structures like weed lines or rocky drop-offs. The best bait for Perch are minnows, with mayfly larvae (wigglers) a close second. Perch have a very firm textured sweet meat and are great eating.

PUMPKINSEED SUNFISH

When fishing for panfish, you will eventually catch a Pumpkinseed Sunfish. They have very colorful bodies with iridescent blue lines and bright orange bellies. Pumpkinseed Sunfish are known by the red spot at the rear of their gill covers. These fish are great fighters. They make a tasty meal when caught from cold clean waters.

BLACK CRAPPIE

Black Crappie is a beautiful fish of glittering silver with dark black blotches over the complete body. These fish tend to school together around weed beds and sunken trees. If you catch one, there are usually more in the area ready to be caught. Minnows are the best bait for Black Crappie.

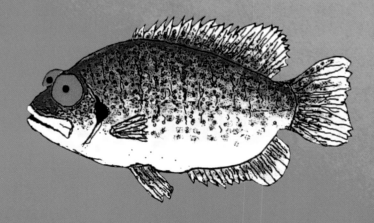

ROCK BASS

Rock Bass, or sometimes called "Red Eyes," are often caught when fishing for Bluegills, Sunfish, or Perch. They have big red eyes and stocky olive brown bodies covered with rows of black spots. When caught, Rock Bass fight hard for a couple seconds and then pull in like dead weight. Though not considered a quality eating fish, they can taste better from a cold clean lake or stream.

GAMEFISH

Usually caught for sport then released. When taken from a clean stream or deep lake, they can be very tasty.

LARGEMOUTH & SMALLMOUTH BASS

Largemouth Bass are olive green color with a blotchy black stripe running down the middle of their bodies and have pearl white bellies. Their mouths extend behind the eyes. Smallmouth Bass are beautiful bronze green color with dark vertical banding across their bodies. Their mouths do NOT extend behind the eyes. Bass like to eat other smaller fish and crayfish. Night crawlers and shiner minnows are excellent baits for Bass. Largemouth and Smallmouth Bass are strong fighters. Smallmouth Bass like to run under your boat when hooked. These gamefish are usually released after the catch, but can be very tasty when taken from a clean cold lake or stream.

NORTHERN PIKE

These fish have long sleek bodies with white spots on a dark green background. Their big heads are full of sharp teeth. Northern Pikes are voracious eaters of fish, frogs, and crayfish. The best baits for these toothy fish are shiner minnows and night crawlers. They are found around weed beds, fallen trees, and rocky structures. Northern Pikes have a very firm tasty meat, but watch out for the bones.

WALLEYE

The Walleye has a long, slender, olive green body with a mix of yellow gold. The pearlescent eyes and the white tip on the lower part of the tail assure that you have caught a Walleye. They eat small fish, crayfish, and mayfly larvae. They are found near drop-offs and weed beds 10 to 20 feet deep. The best bait to use for this fish is a yellow or chartreuse colored jig tipped with a minnow. Trolling a night crawler on a spinner harness is also very effective. Be careful as they have very sharp teeth.

TROUT

Trout are beautiful fish that prefer clean cold waters. There are many species of trout located throughout the world. The Rainbow Trout is one of the most sought after species in North America. Rainbow Trout can be found in clean cold lakes and gravelly streams. These fish have a colorful iridescent pink line running the horizontal length of their silver black spotted bodies with pearl white bellies. Trout feed on insects, insect larvae, minnows, and fish eggs. The average size of an adult river dwelling Rainbow Trout is about 16 inches in length and 2 to 8 pounds in weight.

Steelheads are the same species as the Rainbow Trout. Steelheads live in the ocean or Great Lakes. Because of the difference in their environment, Steelheads can grow much larger and may weigh over 30 pounds. Steelheads differ in color from the river run Rainbow Trout. Steelheads have greyish heads and metallic silver colored bodies. You will need specialized equipment when fishing for Steelheads as they are strong spectacular fighters. Use an 8 to 10 foot rod with a flexible tip and strong backbone. A well built reel with lots of line and a good drag will also be needed.

SALMON

Fishing for Salmon is a popular thrill packed adventure. Salmon are beautiful, muscular, and incredibly strong fighting fish. Pacific and Atlantic Salmon are the two main groups of Salmon found around the United States. There are many species of Salmon. Three popular species of Pacific Salmon are Chinook (Kings), Coho (Silver), and Sockeye (Red). Salmon live in large bodies of either fresh or saltwater. In the spring they swim up rivers to lay their eggs, otherwise known as a "Salmon Run". The species and habitat will determine the type of fishing equipment needed. Salmon are a delicious source of heart healthy protein.

BULLHEAD

Bullheads have big heads, barbels at their mouths, and smooth skin that lack scales. Bullheads have yellowish brown to brownish black bodies with yellow or white bellies. Be careful when handling Bullheads. They have very sharp spines on the dorsal and pectoral fins. They prefer slow moving water in lakes, streams, and ponds. Bullheads are bottom feeding fish. They can tolerate muddy, murky, weedy, and low oxygen content waters. Fishing for them is best after sundown, as they feed at night. Bullheads will eat most anything thrown their way, but night crawlers and worms seem to work the best. Use a medium action rod with 6 pound test clear line on your reel to catch them. When caught from a clean lake or stream, their pinkish meat is a delicacy.

BOWFIN

Bowfin or "Dogfish" are greenish brown in color. The males have a very prominent black "eye spot" on the upper part of their rounded tails. A Dogfish has a large head with a mouthful of sharp teeth. Their muscular bodies have long dorsal fins. Dogfish are not picky eaters and will attack almost any type of bait thrown their way. They give a great fight and could try to bite you. Dogfish are not considered good for eating, but there are some recipes on the web.

CARP

The common carp has a stocky, heavy, humpbacked body covered with large scales. Two barbels are found on each side of their down-turned mouths. Carp are considered bottom feeders, but they do feed on vegetation, seeds, and insects that float on the water surface. Carp can vary in color, but usually have bronze, olive black bodies with silver yellow bellies. Carp are tremendous fighters and are a lot of fun to catch. Use a medium to medium heavy rod with a matching reel that can hold a large amount of 10 to 15 pound test line. Use a small treble hook baited with corn, dough balls, or worms.

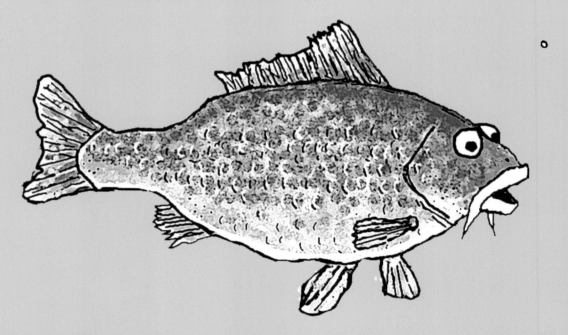

SUPERB SAUTÉED PAN FISH

A 5 star recipe providing a light flavorful batter for all fish

INGREDIENTS

1 cup Cornflake Crumbs

1 cup Whole Wheat Flour

1 ¼ Tablespoon Seasoned Salt

¼ Teaspoon Black Pepper

¼ Teaspoon Ground Basil

1 cup 2% or Whole Milk

1 fresh Egg

Margarine

Place the first five ingredients in a food processor or blender and mix for 15-20 seconds. This blending will make a very fine coating mix. Place the batter in an 8"x 8" square pan. For a thicker more crunchy batter, skip the blending process.

In a separate bowl, mix milk and egg together until completely blended. Add the fish fillets to the milk/ egg mixture and let set for five minutes. Remove the fillets from the milk/egg mixture one at a time and coat with batter on both sides of the fish. Place the battered fish on a plate in the freezer for 5 minute quick chill. This will set the batter for better cooking. Turn burner on to medium heat. Add margarine to a non-stick frying pan, and let it melt as to cover the complete cooking surface. Then cook the fillets on both sides until golden brown. You will need to add additional margarine during the cooking process, in order to keep the fillets from burning.

ENJOY!

TAKE CARE OF YOUR FISH

Fish are an excellent source of protein. They can be delicious and nutritious when taken from cold clean waters. Water quality of the lake or stream has a large impact on the smell and taste of the fish. Fish caught from large, deep, cold lakes and streams during the winter, early spring, and late fall are usually the best for eating. Fresh water fish caught from warm, shallow, weedy, algae prone lakes or streams can smell musty. They can also have a grassy and muddy taste. This is due to organic compounds in the water produced by certain strains of algae and bacteria.

NOT A NIBBLE OR BITE ALL DAY

Fish have a very delicate flesh that needs proper care. When you catch fish you plan to eat, put them directly on ice. Make sure the ice container has a drain. Never put fish in a wire basket hanging in warm surface water. Do not let fish sit in any standing water in a cooler or pail. Bacteria in surface waters and from fish slime can affect the texture and taste of the meat. Cold firm fish are also much easier to clean. Treat fish just like a premium piece of meat that you purchased from your favorite market.

GOING FISHING

CHECK LIST

A LIBRARY CARD IS NOT AN APPROVED FISHING LICENSE

- ☐ FISHING & DRIVERS LICENSES
- ☐ FISHING REGULATIONS
- ☐ RODS & REELS
- ☐ FRESH FISHING LINE
- ☐ HOOKS & LURES & JIGS

- ☐ HOOK SHARPENER
- ☐ TAPE MEASURE
- ☐ TACKLE BOX
- ☐ FRESH LIVE BAIT
- ☐ DEPTH FINDER
- ☐ FISHING NET

DEEP INSIDE HAROLD WONDERED IF HIS WIFE REALLY BELIEVED
THE DOG HAD ORDERED A $500.00 MAGNESIUM ALLOY, MICROMODULE
GEAR SYSTEM BAIT CASTING COMBO

FILLETING FISH

When filleting a fish, make your first two cuts from the top of the head to the tail on both sides of the fish. Follow the back bone and keep the cutting depth above the rib cage. Fish are rounded not flat. These first cuts will make the removal of the meat off the rib bones a simple procedure. Rinse fillets thoroughly with clean water and dry with paper towels. Fish fillets can be kept in the refrigerator for up to 4 days. When freezing fish, vacuum sealing is the recommended method. Wrap the plastic vacuum-sealed bag with aluminium foil to prevent freezer burn. Label and date each package.

HAROLD EXPERIENCED SOME CONFUSION
REGARDING THE SECTION ON PAN FISHING